Chicago Tribune

# BEARS ROAR

## MEET THE MEN WHO PUT THE SWAGGER
## BACK INTO CHICAGO FOOTBALL

No part of this
publication may be
reproduced,
stored in a retrieval
system, or transmitted,
in any form by any
means, electronic,
mechanical,
photocopying, or
otherwise, without
prior written
permission of
the publisher,
Triumph Books,
542 S. Dearborn St.
Suite 750,
Chicago, IL 60605.

This book is available
in quantity at special
discounts for your
group or organization.

For further
information, contact:
Triumph Books
542 S. Dearborn St.
Suite 750
Chicago, IL 60605
Phone: (312) 939-3330
Fax: (312) 663-3557

Printed in the United
States of America
ISBN 13: 978-1-60078-001-1
ISBN 10: 1-60078-001-6

Cover photo:
Jim Prisching
Back cover:
John Smierciak

An unexpected find,
Bernard Berrian hauls in a touchdown
pass over Seattle's Kelly Herndon (31)
and Oliver Celestin.
JIM PRISCHING

Rookie Mark Anderson smashes Matt Leinart, leading to a fumble that Mike Brown ran in for a score against Arizona. JOHN SMIERCIAK

Soldier Field tailgaters party now, but a few hours later they would be disappointed with a 31-13 loss to Miami. E. JASON WAMBSGANS

Not even a season-opening shutout of the Packers can keep one Bears fan from chatting on his cell phone. HEATHER STONE

# Contents

SCOTT STRAZZANTE

*By* DAVID HAUGH

# THE 2006 RISE OF THE BEARS

**T**HEY HAD TO SEE to believe. Only minutes earlier the Bears had become the first team in NFL history to overcome a 20-point deficit without scoring an offensive touchdown in a 24-23 win over the Arizona Cardinals on "Monday Night Football." Now in a jubilant locker room inside University of Phoenix Stadium, giddy Bears players and coaches gathered around the big-screen TV to watch replays of the highlights they had just supplied. Mike Brown scooping up a fumble caused by Mark Anderson and returning it for a touchdown.

Brian Urlacher ripping the ball out of Edgerrin James' arms and Charles Tillman picking it up to run for another TD. Devin Hester turning the middle of the field into his personal express lane with the game-winning punt return.

As the replays filled the screen again and again, the Bears shook their heads and hugged each other and lingered longer than usual in their uniforms before hitting the showers. It was a feeling nobody wanted to wash away, a night nobody in that room wanted to end, an image that was the most indelible in a season full of them.

It marked the moment the players and coaches sensed they were part of something special.

Now the Bears knew how the rest of Chicago felt.

The comparisons to 1985 already had begun at that point. Fair or not, it was inevitable; the city had not enjoyed a Super Bowl champion since that season and the White Sox winning the World Series in 2005 convinced people in Chicago that anything was possible.

After the 2006 Bears performance in the first month of the season, some carried-away fans started thinking a Super Bowl berth was probable.

They pointed to the way the Bears overwhelmed their first four opponents in a way that statistically was more dominating than the '85 team that set the franchise standard. They looked at how parity had diluted the NFC.

But Lovie Smith is no Mike Ditka and tried his level-headed best to discourage any historical links to '85 and keep the increased attention from becoming a distraction.

An offense scoring at a record pace only made that task trickier. So did Smith himself by uncharacteristically calling the Bears a team of destiny after their "Monday Night Miracle," as some players started referring to the Arizona win.

In reality, good execution had more to do with it than good fortune.

The biggest difference early in the season was quarterback Rex Grossman, the NFC's Player of the Month in September and America's media darling in October. When Grossman was bad, as he was against Arizona and Miami, he made some fans long for Kyle Orton and clamor for Brian Griese. But when Grossman is as good as he was for most of the first half, he can give the Bears the look of an authentic Super Bowl contender.

It helped that the Bears' veteran offensive line made the pocket roomy and comfortable for Grossman whenever he dropped back to pass.

Wide receiver Bernard Berrian also emerged as a legitimate deep threat. Tight end Desmond Clark gave the team its first viable downfield weapon at the position since Ditka 40 years earlier. Running back Thomas Jones ran well enough to hold off Cedric Benson, who publicly pined for more playing time.

Defensively, Urlacher dominated like he was determined to win a second straight NFL Defensive Player of the Year Award and had a 25-tackle game against Arizona that sparked talk about Urlacher's Hall of Fame credentials. What Urlacher didn't get to, fellow linebacker Lance Briggs did.

Tommie Harris kept the mood light in the locker room and the pressure heavy on quarterbacks. Anderson, a rookie pass rusher taken in the fifth round, burst onto the scene and into the backfield like a 21st Century Richard Dent.

The secondary, depleted by the season-ending injury to Brown against Arizona, received its biggest early season boost from $21 million free-agent nickel back Ricky Manning Jr.

The only other new defensive back who had a bigger, quicker impact was rookie Hester with game-changing punt returns for TDs against Green Bay and Arizona.

Then there was kicker Robbie Gould, as affable as he was accurate, making history less than a year after making the team five games into the '05 season.

This was the way general manager Jerry Angelo always envisioned his master plan unfolding, even during the roughest part of Angelo's five years in Chicago when he faced criticism after the 2003 season for taking almost three weeks to find Dick Jauron's replacement.

When Angelo finally introduced the Bears' new head coach Jan. 15, 2004, at Halas Hall, Smith boldly announced his intentions from Day One: Beat Green Bay, capture the NFC North and win the Super Bowl. There was stifled laughter in the crowd.

Nobody was laughing less than three full seasons into Smith's tenure. Except in the Bears' locker room where, on nights like the one in Arizona, they have had a hard time containing their glee.

The architect and the craftsman: General manager Jerry Angelo built the team, and coach Lovie Smith has won with it. JIM PRISCHING

*By* DAVID HAUGH

# HOW THE BEARS WERE BUILT

N THE MIDST OF TALKING about how much he has changed since taking over as the Bears' general manager in June 2001, Jerry Angelo used his hands for emphasis as he sat in his Halas Hall office.

"I've had a metamorphosis," Angelo said.

He gestured toward the practice field, where Angelo could see a Bears team he had crafted by complementing a defense heavy on draft picks with an offense loaded with high-priced free agents.

He motioned to the giant board where hundreds of college prospects were arranged on the wall the same way diamonds in the rough Mark Anderson and Danieal Manning had been a year ago.

Angelo knocked over a bottle of water but just kept talking.

There was a time when he might have apologized, wondered whether somebody might make fun of him or stopped to dwell on the spill. But with that insignificant office mishap, Angelo unwittingly drove home the point he was trying to make:

The man who used to sweat the small stuff no longer allows little things to blur the big picture as he sees it.

Angelo has stopped letting previous missteps affect the next move forward. He started drawing his own modern blueprint for an NFL team instead of following the dated specifications he had used to help build winners in Tampa Bay, New York and Dallas.

For example, he signed a backup quarterback, Brian Griese, after seeing in 2005 how his failure to do so had limited the Bears for a second straight season.

He still operates by the book. But he has expanded the glossary.

"As you get older, you go one of two ways: Your blinders go like this (turning his hands in) or like this (opening them)," Angelo said. "You have to ask yourself: 'Am I going to stay this course and take not necessarily the path of least resistance but [an easier one]? Or are you going to turn over those rocks?'

"I didn't always understand the big picture until I got here and was thrown into situations. I could have stayed that course. Or I could have said, 'I have to find alternative ways,' and that personally is what happened."

Sometime in the year before Angelo hired Lovie Smith to replace Dick Jauron as coach in January 2004, he remembers a

# HOW EACH PLAYER
# BECAME A BEAR

 **NFL DRAFT**    **FREE AGENCY**   **TRADED FROM ANOTHER TEAM**

**96** Alex Brown, DE (ROUND 4)

▲ DEFENSE

▼ OFFENSE/
SPECIAL
TEAMS

| | | | | |
|---|---|---|---|---|
| | **54** Brian Urlacher, LB (ROUND 1) | | **60** Terrence Metcalf, G (ROUND 3) |
| **57** Olin Kreutz, C (ROUND 3) | **30** Mike Brown, SS (ROUND 2) | | **29** Adrian Peterson, RB (ROUND 6) |
| **65** Patrick Mannelly, LS (ROUND 6) | **70** Alfonso Boone, DT | **4** Brad Maynard, P | **85** John Gilmore, TE |

| | 1998 | 1999* | 2000 | 2001 | 2002 |
|---|---|---|---|---|---|
| Mark Hatley (GENERAL MANAGER 1997–2000) | | | | Jerry Angelo (GENERAL MANAGER SINCE 2001) | |
| Dave Wannstedt (COACH 1993–98) | | Dick Jauron (COACH 1999–2003) | | | |

\* NO PLAYERS ON ROSTER FROM CLASS OF '99

CHICAGO TRIBUNE GRAPHIC BY CHUCK BURKE

conversation with a former NFL general manager whose name he did not disclose. It turned into some of the best advice he ever got.

"I asked, 'What did you learn?' He said, 'I didn't take advantage of the free-agent market based on what I see going on now,' " Angelo said. "That kind of stuck with me."

Angelo's reputation for working on draft-driven teams helped him land the Bears job. He spent 14 years in the front office at Tampa Bay, where drafting Warren Sapp, Mike Alstott and John Lynch helped change the direction of the franchise. Be-

fore that he spent his formative years scouting for the Cowboys and Giants when building via the draft was the only option before free agency changed the league in 1993.

Eight of 11 starters on the Bears' offense signed as free agents, the most notable being left tackle John Tait and running back Thomas Jones in 2004 and receiver Muhsin Muhammad and right tackle Fred Miller in 2005. The draft picks are impact ones: receiver Bernard Berrian and quarterback Rex Grossman.

Conversely, nine of 11 defensive starters are Bears draft picks. But defensive

end Adewale Ogunleye, acquired in a trade with Miami in 2004, might have been Angelo's boldest move.

"When I look at our football team, I see we didn't stay down a chosen path, and that shows strength," Angelo said.

To Angelo, a roster mixed with free-agent steals and draft-day finds reflects organizational progress as much as anything. But nothing confirms it more than Arena Football League reclamation project Rashied Davis.

"If you want to look at one player who best exemplifies who we are as an

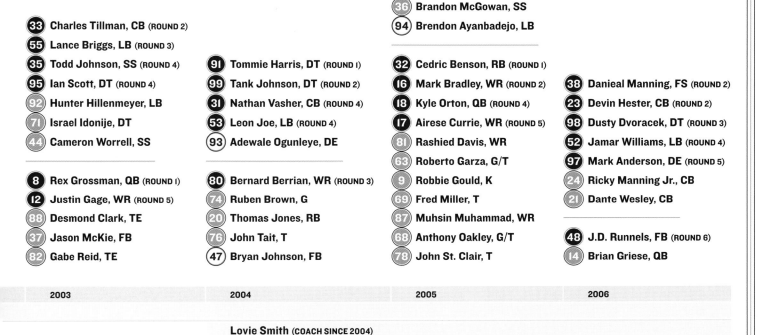

**(33)** Charles Tillman, CB (ROUND 2)
**(55)** Lance Briggs, LB (ROUND 3)
**(35)** Todd Johnson, SS (ROUND 4)
**(95)** Ian Scott, DT (ROUND 4)
**(92)** Hunter Hillenmeyer, LB
**(71)** Israel Idonije, DT
**(44)** Cameron Worrell, SS

**(8)** Rex Grossman, QB (ROUND 1)
**(12)** Justin Gage, WR (ROUND 5)
**(88)** Desmond Clark, TE
**(37)** Jason McKie, FB
**(82)** Gabe Reid, TE

**(91)** Tommie Harris, DT (ROUND 1)
**(99)** Tank Johnson, DT (ROUND 2)
**(31)** Nathan Vasher, CB (ROUND 4)
**(53)** Leon Joe, LB (ROUND 4)
**(93)** Adewale Ogunleye, DE

**(80)** Bernard Berrian, WR (ROUND 3)
**(74)** Ruben Brown, G
**(20)** Thomas Jones, RB
**(76)** John Tait, T
**(47)** Bryan Johnson, FB

**(46)** Chris Harris, FS (ROUND 6)
**(64)** Rod Wilson, LB (ROUND 7)
**(90)** Antonio Garay, DT
**(36)** Brandon McGowan, SS
**(94)** Brendon Ayanbadejo, LB

**(32)** Cedric Benson, RB (ROUND 1)
**(16)** Mark Bradley, WR (ROUND 2)
**(18)** Kyle Orton, QB (ROUND 4)
**(17)** Airese Currie, WR (ROUND 5)
**(81)** Rashied Davis, WR
**(63)** Roberto Garza, G/T
**(9)** Robbie Gould, K
**(69)** Fred Miller, T
**(87)** Muhsin Muhammad, WR
**(68)** Anthony Oakley, G/T
**(78)** John St. Clair, T

**(38)** Danieal Manning, FS (ROUND 2)
**(23)** Devin Hester, CB (ROUND 2)
**(98)** Dusty Dvoracek, DT (ROUND 3)
**(52)** Jamar Williams, LB (ROUND 4)
**(97)** Mark Anderson, DE (ROUND 5)
**(24)** Ricky Manning Jr., CB
**(21)** Dante Wesley, CB

**(48)** J.D. Runnels, FB (ROUND 6)
**(14)** Brian Griese, QB

| 2003 | 2004 | 2005 | 2006 |
|------|------|------|------|

**Lovie Smith** (COACH SINCE 2004)

organization, use him," Angelo said. "If somebody would have brought up an Arena League player to me 10 years ago, I would have laughed. I would have said we have enough to do without looking at a foreign league that doesn't play our brand of football.

"But we looked at him, brought him in and treated him like a draft pick. The guy has turned into a pretty good player."

Gil Brandt has known Angelo since the day Angelo walked into his office unannounced and uninvited in 1980 looking for a job. Brandt, an architect of the great Cowboys teams of the 1970s, still follows

the Bears as NFL.com's senior analyst. He notices similarities to the brash fellow he hired 26 years ago.

"He has some of the most tremendous work habits you'll ever see," Brandt said. "He'll ... do whatever it takes to know a player."

That approach trickles down to Angelo's staff of six college scouts. A former scout himself, Angelo initially structured his scouts' schedules the way his used to be: Get to a school, get out and go see as many prospects as possible.

But over time, Angelo saw more value in having his scouts stay as long as neces-

sary to get to really know a player, even if it meant seeing fewer prospects.

"I tell them I'm not worried about the player you miss," Angelo said. "Make sure you know him."

Angelo linked the Bears' success through the draft and free agency with an exhaustive off-season self-evaluation process that involves interviewing coaches on the type of players they want.

"We break it down so there's a clear picture in every scout's mind what a Bear looks like," Angelo said.

The look of the Bears organization seldom has been in sharper focus.

# MEET
# THE BEARS

**Charge! Tight end Desmond Clark leads the Bears out of the tunnel before the ill-fated Miami game.**
E. JASON WAMBSGANS

# LOVIE SMITH
## HEAD COACH: the loyal boss

One day last summer in the small east Texas town of Big Sandy, they named a street after Lovie Smith. That is where the road the Bears hope to travel to the Super Bowl truly begins.

The Bears coach learned all about football and life in his hometown, where it can be hard to tell the difference. He became skilled at handling adversity as the son of an alcoholic father and at overcoming long odds from watching his mother fight diabetes, which eventually took her sight.

Most of all, Smith developed a love for a sport that has made him wealthy and for a community he'll never forget.

His human touch and folksiness have grown on Bears players, who appreciate the way Smith maintains the same demeanor, win or lose. He is the anti-Ditka, a coach more comfortable in the background than the spotlight.

"He's not a wishy-washy guy, and that goes a long way with players," guard Ruben Brown says.

Adds cornerback Charles Tillman: "You have his back; he has our back."

That kind of loyalty developed quickly after Smith was actually the second choice to replace Dick Jauron in 2004. After Nick Saban turned down the job, Smith won over the Bears' brass with his straightforward, honest nature.

Smith identified the Bears-Packers rivalry as the team's No. 1 goal in his introductory press conference. He listed the second and third objectives as winning the NFC North and the Super Bowl, respectively. Initially, such bold talk for a team that hadn't won a playoff game since 1995 drew scoffs. But well into Smith's third season, nobody's laughing.

Smith has changed the culture at Halas Hall by stressing speed and putting players on weight-loss plans, emphasizing turnovers and stripping the football, and being willing to change personnel to increase accountability.

Players also respect the way Smith has kept his status as the NFL's lowest-paid coach at $1.35 million from becoming a distraction. Smith has insisted coaching the Bears has never been about the money.

"I don't know if I'm perfect for the job," he likes to say, "but I know the job is definitely perfect for me."

— *David Haugh*

Lovie Smith has had many reasons to smile this season and undoubtedly is hoping for more in the playoffs. JIM PRISCHING

The sweat and toil of training camp in Bourbonnais has paid off for coach Lovie Smith and his Bears. NUCCIO DINUZZO

# THE DEFENSE

Tank Johnson (left), Tommie Harris and Adewale Ogunleye help make the Bears' defensive line an unpleasant place for opponents.
HEATHER STONE

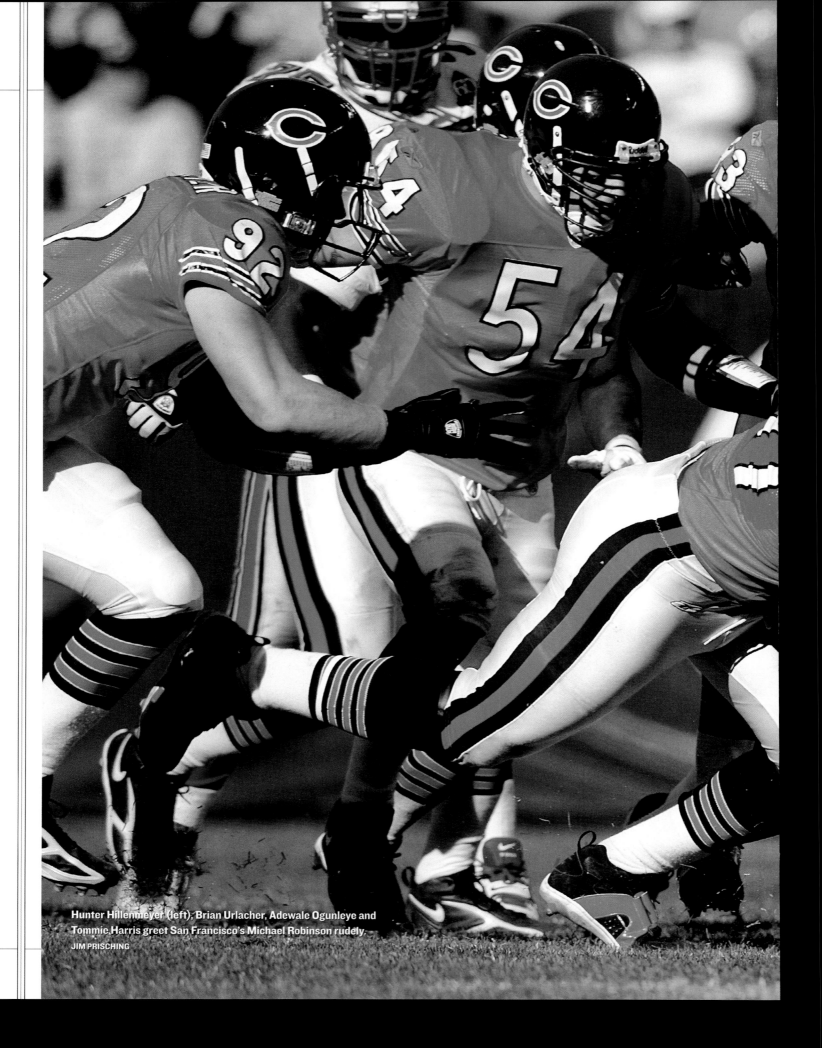

Hunter Hillenmeyer (left), Brian Urlacher, Adewale Ogunleye and Tommie Harris greet San Francisco's Michael Robinson rudely.
JIM PRISCHING

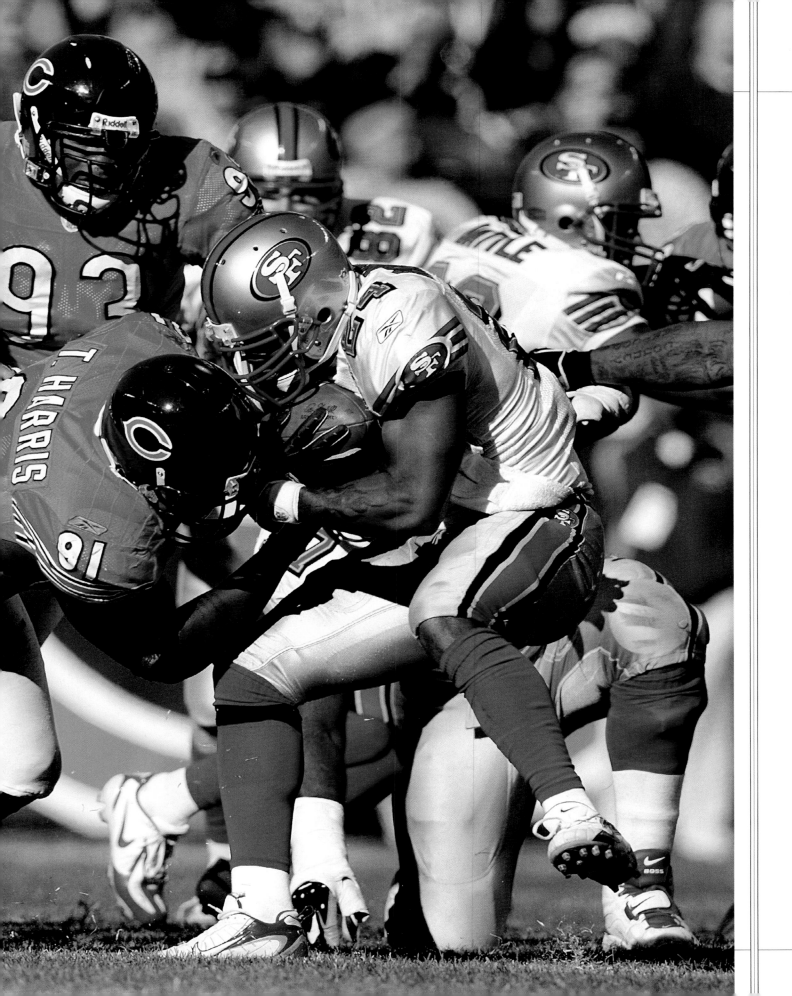

# RON RIVERA
## DEFENSIVE COORDINATOR: the pedigreed commander

A second-round linebacker drafted by the Bears in 1984 after linebacker Wilber Marshall, Ron Rivera also was head coach Lovie Smith's second choice as defensive coordinator behind former Tampa Bay assistant Rod Marinelli, Smith's best friend in coaching. But Rivera's defenses with the Bears have proved second to none in the NFL.

After playing under Bears defensive co-ordinators Buddy Ryan and Vince Tobin and linebackers coach Dave McGinnis, Rivera worked as a TV analyst before joining Dave Wannstedt as the Bears' defensive quality-control coach in 1997. He left when Andy Reid took over the Philadelphia Eagles, where Rivera was linebackers coach under defensive coordinator Jim Johnson.

The combination of influences exposed Rivera to primarily attack-style defenses that thrive on disruption and turnovers.

"It's a lot of fun for guys when they know your philosophy is to attack," says Rivera, 44. "But it's not just that you attack. It's knowing when to attack and putting them in a position where you can attack. What I'm looking for is to always put our guys in the best possible situations so we can attack."

Born in Ft. Ord, Calif., where his dad was a military officer, Rivera calls himself "an Army brat" who spent a lot of his youth in Panama before moving back to the U.S.

Though he has installed primarily the defensive scheme Smith brought from Tampa Bay and St. Louis, Rivera has placed his own stamp on it by making calls from the coaches' box and challenging players with his own outgoing and expressive personality.

Rivera was among the finalists for the head-coaching jobs in Green Bay and St. Louis after the 2005 season and is expected to be among the front-runners for openings again after this season.

"I have aspirations of being an NFL head coach," he says. "I've made that clear."

— *Don Pierson*

The face of the Bears?

Olin Kreutz laughed when asked if he fit that description after he signed a three-year contract extension this autumn that all but assures the perennial All-Pro center will retire a Bear.

"I don't think I'm the face of the Bears," Kreutz said. "That obviously belongs to Brian Urlacher."

Though it took a position change after a successful college career as a safety to get Urlacher to what is seemingly his birthright at middle linebacker, few question that he is now where he belongs, stalking ballcarriers with a hunger that is all Bear.

A native of Lovington, N.M., a football-crazy southwestern desert town of about 9,500 surrounded by some 17,000 oil rigs, Urlacher came to the Bears as the ninth pick in the 2000 draft. He wasted little time making a big impression.

The third Bear to be named Defensive Rookie of the Year and the second Bears rookie to lead the team in tackles, Urlacher made the Pro Bowl that first year and in each of his first four seasons.

That achievement put him in the company of Rick Casares, Dick Butkus, Mike Ditka and Gale Sayers. But it was 2005, when Urlacher made his fifth Pro Bowl team and was named the Associated Press Defensive Player of the Year, that he seemed to officially take his place as one of the premier players of his generation.

Discussing a notable failure in 2002, Urlacher quickly flashed back to his first training camp with the Bears.

"I was playing [strong-side linebacker] and Rosie [Colvin] beat me out," he said. "Hard as I tried, I just couldn't play [there]. Obviously they found out I wasn't very good and moved me to the middle, and everything else has been great."

As for taking his place among the dynasty of great Bears linebackers, Urlacher is humble.

"There is a great tradition here of linebackers and defense, so it's an honor to play here," he says. "But I've got a long way to go to get where most of those guys were."

— *Melissa Isaacson*

# 54
# BRIAN URLACHER
## LINEBACKER: the unequivocal leader

During his off-the-charts second half at Arizona, Brian Urlacher goes airborne to bring down Edgerrin James. JIM PRISCHING

Opposing offenses' tendencies are never far out of the sight of linebackers Brian Urlacher (left) and Hunter Hillenmeyer.

JIM PRISCHING

It's no stretch to include Brian Urlacher among the most outstanding players in Bears history.

NUCCIO DINUZZO

# CONVERSATION
## with Brian Urlacher

The 6-foot-4-inch, 258-pounder is from Lovington, N.M. He played college ball at New Mexico, where he was an outside linebacker and free safety on defense, a wide receiver on offense and a return specialist.

**Favorite pro team growing up:** "I hate to say it, but it was the Cowboys. Growing up in New Mexico, they were about the only thing we got to watch on TV."

**Favorite player growing up:** "Darren Woodson. He was a big safety. I thought I was a big safety, so I kind of related to him a little bit."

**Hardest adjustment from safety to linebacker:** "Just learning the defense. Athletically, I think it wasn't that much of a change. It was just playing with the linemen. At safety, I was playing in a bunch of space. Now I had to get down with the linemen, using my hands and learning the defense."

**Toughest one-on-one matchup you've ever faced:** "Everyone is good in the NFL, we know that. I used to have problems with Matt Birk, the center from Minnesota, back when they ran a different offense."

**Favorite team right now not named Bears:** "I'll be politically correct and say the Bulls. And the Lobos."

**Best advice you ever received:** "Just 'Play hard.' Good things will come your way when you fly to the football."

# 55

# LANCE BRIGGS
## LINEBACKER: the underrated star

Lance Briggs has quietly become a Bears institution. Emphasis on quietly, because his career has played out in the shadow of Brian Urlacher.

Until last season.

Urlacher edged him for the team lead in tackles with 171 to his 170, but Briggs finally was accorded some overdue respect when he was voted to his first Pro Bowl and selected as a first-team All-Pro.

The Bears linebacker became the only NFL player to return an interception for a touchdown in each of his first three seasons. He added another pick this season but had to settle for an 18-yard return that didn't reach the end zone.

When the Bears selected Briggs in the third round out of Arizona in 2003, Urlacher said he considered Briggs the rookie of the year, in part because Briggs played all out—and well—every week. That has not changed.

"[Urlacher] told me not to worry so much, have fun and it'll take care of itself," Briggs says. "He said he did a lot of similar things when he was a rookie. Once he learned, he just flew around."

Briggs won a starting job at strong-side linebacker four games into his rookie season and finished with 81 tackles. In the 2004 off-season he switched to weak-side linebacker and more than doubled his total of tackles at a position that gave him more freedom to work in space.

His speed and instincts allowed him to stay in on passing downs, and he has gotten progressively better against receivers. After a combined nine pass breakups his first two seasons, he had 13 last year.

"I realized to start on this defense, you have to learn so you get to the point you feel comfortable," Briggs says. "You can't be worrying about making mistakes. You have to just let it go."

— *John Mullin*

# 24
# RICKY MANNING JR.
## CORNERBACK: the punishing hitter

The Bears bragged all off-season about returning all 22 starters. But that statistic overlooked the addition of a player whose role makes him, in essence, the 23rd starter. And he wears jersey No. 24.

Ricky Manning Jr. signed a $21 million free-agent contract to play nickelback after three seasons in Carolina, where he started 26 games. The Bears place a premium on the nickel job because they use five defensive backs more than a third of the time to combat three-receiver sets, and they needed to replace Jerry Azumah, who retired.

Enter Manning, ideally suited to face slot receivers because of his nimble feet and physical style. He stands only 5 feet 9 inches tall but frustrates bigger receivers by roughing them up.

Manning quickly became such an integral part of the defense that much of the early season was devoted to discussing how badly the Bears would miss him if he faced NFL discipline for his no-contest plea in September to a felony assault charge stemming from an incident last spring at a Los Angeles area restaurant.

Sentiments of support echoed through the locker room for a player who fit in immediately with his fellow Bears.

Strong backing from his teammates and coach Lovie Smith during the fallout from the no-contest plea kept Manning's confidence at a level as high as his play. It did not take him long to show the same knack for finding the football that he showed in Carolina, where he picked off four passes in the postseason as a rookie in 2003.

That was the same year Manning left a lasting impression on Smith by intercepting a St. Louis pass in an NFC playoff game for the Panthers when Smith was the Rams' defensive coordinator. Then last season at Soldier Field, Manning picked off Kyle Orton during a regular-season game at Soldier Field.

"He's a tough player," Smith says. "I've known Ricky for a while. He had as much to do with Carolina beating us my last year in St. Louis as anyone that day."

He has had as much to do with the Bears' secondary making a difference this season as any player, new or old.

"This is home now," Manning says.

— *David Haugh*

# 91

# TOMMIE HARRIS

## DEFENSIVE TACKLE: the maturing kid

When Lovie Smith arrived to coach the Bears in 2004, one of the first orders of franchise business was to recast the team, particularly the defense. The idea was to move away from the size of the previous defensive system and toward speed.

The biggest step in that direction was drafting Tommie Harris with the 14th pick that year. The 6-foot-3-inch, 295-pounder had been an All-American at Oklahoma, where his teammates included current Bears Mark Bradley, Dusty Dvoracek and J.D. Runnels.

Harris quickly established himself with 3½ sacks his rookie season and was voted the Brian Piccolo Award by his teammates, an honor based more on character than on football. Harris has shown that he is not only a character but also has plenty of it.

Last off-season Harris journeyed with former NFL players Lee Roy and Dewey Selmon to Liberia, where they helped build a school for an orphanage in a war-torn region of that country. The action helped not only the people it served but also the young

men involved in making it happen.

"I am a young man, not a grown man, in a grown-man's business," Harris says. "I have to learn right now and learn more and more, and I think I'm doing a pretty good job learning how to keep up with everybody else. Now I want to excel in what I'm doing, my business [affairs], my athleticism. I want to be the greatest in both."

Harris is an integral figure on the Bears' defensive line. He is among the quickest linemen in the NFL, and his assignment is to get through his gap and disrupt offenses.

Harris, voted to the Pro Bowl after last season, worked not only on his football but also on establishing his sense of perspective in a game where that is not always easy.

"I had a couple talks with people and put my mind back into perspective," Harris says. "But it's bigger than the money. I owe this game, and Jesus Christ, so much respect because they have given me so much to let me be where I am today."

— *John Mullin*

# CONVERSATION
## with Tommie Harris

The 2003 Lombardi Award winner at Oklahoma as the nation's best interior lineman is from Killeen, Texas. He is a cousin of Jacksonville Jaguars tackle Stockar McDougle and Philadelphia Eagles defensive end Jerome McDougle.

**Favorite pro team growing up:** "Tampa Bay Buccaneers."

**Favorite college team growing up:** "Florida State."

**Toughest rivalry you've been a part of:** "Oklahoma-Texas."

**Favorite non-football sport to play:** "PlayStation."

**To watch:** "Pool."

**Favorite player growing up:** "Reggie White."

**What's on the iPod when you work out?** "I like a lot of up-tempo stuff. Canton Jones. Kurt Franklin. Just different up-tempo stuff."

**Toughest one-on-one matchup you've ever faced:** "There is none. There's none. … Eh, Larry Allen."

**Favorite team right now not named Bears:** "Bulls."

**Best advice you ever received:** " 'What you do in your off time will affect your on time.' 'Hard work beats talent when talent doesn't work hard.' 'Character is what's displayed when no one else is watching.' I have a whole bunch of 'em."

**Man of the people: Tommie Harris signs autographs before practice during training camp in Bourbonnais.** SCOTT STRAZZANTE

# 96
# ALEX BROWN
## DEFENSIVE END: the focused warrior

It was the night after the first three rounds of the 2002 NFL draft, and Alex Brown was in no mood to be consoled, even by his fiance—now his wife—Karimar.

"She kept asking me, 'What's wrong?'" Brown says. "And I said, 'Will you please stop asking me what's wrong? You know what's wrong. I wanted to go today.'"

A talented, some would even have said gifted, defensive end out of Florida, Brown had been cursed by the rap that he sometimes took plays off. So Karimar had little to offer.

"Can I do anything to help you?" she asked.

"The only thing that will help me," sighed Brown, "is if I'm drafted by the Bears tomorrow."

Four years later, Brown has few regrets about the way things turned out. Now an anchor on one of the most respected defensive units in the NFL, Brown says it's harder to fight perceptions than any opponent.

"I think it's tough if you're not a strong-minded person, if you let things get at you or let things bother you that really don't matter, because everything is going to be said by the way you go out and play," he said. "For me, it was just going out and doing the things I've always done. I always thought that I played hard. I love football."

A product of White Springs, Fla., a rural town of about 850 near the Florida-Georgia border, Brown was raised on a farm and learned early that there was no shortcut around hard work. When it came to football, however, it was pure joy.

"I never thought I wouldn't make it," he says. "I never had the dream of being a doctor or a comedian or being anything else. Football, that was it."

He still thinks about where he was drafted: 104th.

"I want to know [four] years later, why did you take that guy before me?" he says. "That's my only question. But it's not really that important because I'm here and I've accomplished some things, though not nearly enough.

"I want to win the Super Bowl, so until we win that, I'm definitely not satisfied. I don't really need individual things. A Super Bowl would be the ultimate prize for me."

*— Melissa Isaacson*

# 33
# CHARLES TILLMAN
## CORNERBACK: the physical presence

Cornerback is arguably the toughest position in the NFL, and Charles "Peanut" Tillman has experienced his share of ups and downs in his eventful career with the Bears.

During training camp before this season, Tillman talked about his goal for 2006.

"Be more consistent. I can't be so up and down like a roller coaster," said Tillman, whose poor play against premier wide receiver Steve Smith was a major factor in the Bears' disappointing loss to Carolina in the playoffs after last season.

"Last year I was high one minute and low the next. I just want to stay even."

Bears defensive backs coach Steven Wilks believes Tillman has all the physical tools to succeed.

"He's a big, physical guy, and not everybody talks about his speed, but he has pretty good speed," Wilks says. "He's real physical at the line of scrimmage. He does a great job once he gets his hands on the receivers. He's good at shedding a block and making tackles. And he has the range to cover a lot of ground. Overall, he has everything you want in a left corner."

A second-round selection, 35th overall, by the Bears in the 2003 draft, Tillman has accepted the daunting challenge after being a four-year starter at Louisiana-Lafayette. He was an All-American as a senior and a two-time All-Sun Belt selection.

At 6 feet 1 inch and 196 pounds, Tillman also played free safety in college. He accounted for 284 career tackles as a collegian, including two sacks, and had 12 interceptions. He also recovered seven fumbles and blocked three punts.

After joining the Bears, Tillman was named NFL Rookie of the Year and an All-Pro by Sports Illustrated and received Football Digest's NFL Defensive Rookie of the Year honor.

He intercepted a career-high five passes in 2005, returning them for 172 yards. He ranked second in the NFL by averaging 34.4 yards per return.

Tillman also set a Bears record for the longest non-scoring return when he ran back an interception 95 yards last season against Green Bay. It was the fourth-longest interception return in club history.

— *Fred Mitchell*

# 97

# MARK ANDERSON
## DEFENSIVE END: the fiery rookie

Defensive end Mark Anderson is about nothing if not improvement. That's fortunate for him and the Bears.

For most of training camp, the fifth-round draft choice was a spectator, side-lined with a hamstring injury that limited his roster chances to questionable, maybe even doubtful.

Without a chance to prove himself, his options were coming down to the practice squad.

Then he got his chance in the exhibition game at Cleveland, and his play made enough of a statement for him to make the 53-man roster.

"There was definitely a lot riding on [the Cleveland game]," Anderson says. "I just tried to go out and do what I do best and play hard all the time, hoping it'd turn out the way it did."

It has turned out better than he and the Bears reasonably could have expected. Playing primarily as a backup to Alex Brown and Adewale Ogunleye, Anderson was pushing for NFL Defensive Rookie of the Year honors by midseason, leading the team in sacks.

But improving has been a habit with Anderson. He was voted the Ozzie Newsome Most Improved Freshman at Alabama and then earned the Crimson Tide's Billy Newsome Most Improved Defensive Lineman Award the next year. In his senior year, he collected 7½ sacks in 12 games, matching his midyear NFL total and more than the total for his previous three Alabama seasons combined.

He still remembers his first sack. It came as a sixth-grader in a flag-football game.

Harris recalls it as "a straight speed rush, just go. I just ran, had no assignment or anything. I just got back there, and I've been doing it for a while."

His role model?

"When I was coming up, it was Reggie White," Anderson says. "I just liked the way he played, hard all the time, and I tried to model my game after that. I figured that was a good model."

— *John Mullin*

# CONVERSATION
## with Mark Anderson

Anderson is a 6-foot-4-inch, 255-pound speed rusher out of Alabama, from which he graduated with a degree in consumer science. In high school he played receiver as well.

**Favorite pro team growing up:** "Lions."
**Favorite college team growing up:** "Alabama."
**Favorite non-football sport to play:** "Basketball."
**To watch:** "Basketball."
**Favorite player growing up:** "Barry Sanders."
**What's on the iPod when you work out?** "Local stuff from back home. … My homeboy got a rap; I got him on my iPod."
**Toughest one-on-one matchup you've ever faced:** "I don't know, everybody's good. Maybe my brother, like when we're playin' one-on-one basketball. I don't want to give anybody credit right now."
**Favorite game you've ever played in:** "Senior Bowl."
**Favorite game you've watched as a fan:** "Oklahoma-Oklahoma State, 2001."
**Toughest loss you've ever had as a player:** "State semifinals in high school; Auburn any year."
**Favorite team right now not named Bears:** "LeBron's squad."
**Best advice you ever received:** "Keep God first."

J.P. Losman is abused by Mark Anderson, who hits the Bills quarterback and jars the ball loose.

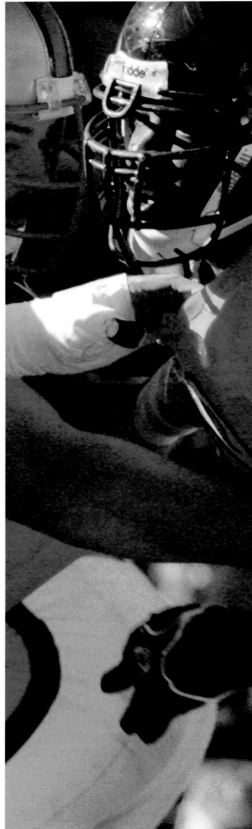

Mark Anderson (right, with Tank Johnson)
has gotten off to a stellar start for the Bears.
E. JASON WAMBSGANS

# 31
# NATHAN VASHER
## CORNERBACK: the intimidating interceptor

Nathan Vasher's signature NFL moment, a 108-yard touchdown return of a missed San Francisco field goal in 2005, already has been commemorated in the Pro Football Hall of Fame. But the affable Bears cornerback has so much more to offer.

"I was feeling like I was running the 400 meters out there," Vasher said after returning Joe Nedney's errant 51-yard attempt at Soldier Field. "I just fell into the end zone. The NFL has been around a long time. For my name to be at the top of that [list] is truly an honor."

Not too shabby for a fourth-round selection who went as the 110th overall pick in the 2004 NFL draft. He led the Bears with five interceptions as a rookie and with eight last season, which ended with a nice perk:

his first trip to the Pro Bowl.

Vasher's role has taken on more significance with the season-ending injury to safety Mike Brown.

"We're definitely better when [Brown] is out there, but I have confidence in the guys to step up and make just as many plays," Vasher says.

The 5-foot-10-inch, 180-pound cornerback out of Texas continues to be a major weapon as a pass defender and interceptor. Vasher's record-breaking return in 2005 should have come as no surprise. He was a fleet wide receiver as well as a defensive back for the Longhorns.

Vasher was a starter at strong safety as well as cornerback for Texas. He intercepted 17 passes in his collegiate career, tying

the school record. He also was named an All-American as a punt returner in 2001.

The third-year Bear entered the 2006 season with 13 career interceptions, including eight in 2005. That was just two shy of the club record set by Mark Carrier when he had 10 interceptions in 1990.

Vasher combined with Charles Tillman to pick off 13 passes in 2005. That tied for the NFL's third-most interceptions by a cornerback tandem. And it was the most by a Bears duo since 1990, when Donnell Woolford had three to augment Carrier's 10.

Vasher continues to pursue that rare acknowledgment as a shut-down corner in the NFL, which only comes with experience and excellence.

— *Fred Mitchell*

# 93

# ADEWALE OGUNLEYE

## DEFENSIVE END: the driven defender

For Adewale Ogunleye, making a name for himself would seem to be a given. But it wasn't until after his first, and as yet only, Pro Bowl start in 2003 that he seemed truly content.

Traded to the Bears from the Miami Dolphins in 2004, one year after leading the AFC with 15 sacks and four years after entering the NFL as an undrafted free agent, Ogunleye is one of the undisputed leaders on a defense loaded with them.

But he does not allow himself to forget how it all started, when a knee injury his senior year at Indiana caused his stock to plummet, pushing him all the way out of the draft.

"That always drives me because it just showed how people were so quick to abandon you when things got rough," he said in 2004. "It almost made me bitter a little when I chose to stay in college one more year, and then you get hurt and everybody turns their back on you.

"I use it to make me better. It's always in the back of my mind."

A native of New York and the great-great-grandson of the former king of Nigeria, Ogunleye said he had to continue to win people over even after signing a six-year deal worth $33.4 million with the Bears.

"It's crazy with life," he says. "You feel like you always have to prove yourself no matter what. Even when I signed a big contract, I had to prove I was worth it. Even though I really had the pedigree in the bag years before and I put my time in, people still want you to show it."

In Miami, the dig was that Ogunleye profited from teams double-teaming Jason Taylor at the other defensive end position.

"I didn't want to buy into what people were saying, but I wanted to prove I could do it without [Taylor]," Ogunleye says. "If I continue to stay healthy and play well, it will show I don't need anybody."

Indeed, Ogunleye and Alex Brown are now considered one of the top defensive end tandems in the NFL. Says Ogunleye:

"When I first got here, I said to Alex, `You and I, we've got the chance to be great.' And we're starting to play like that. Ultimately, you always want to prove people wrong."

— *Melissa Isaacson*

# THE OFFENSE

Commanding respect in the huddle has allowed quarterback Rex Grossman to keep the offense purring. E. JASON WAMBSGANS

Arena Football League refugee
Rashied Davis has exceeded
expectations at the wide
receiver position.
NUCCIO DINUZZO

Keeping the lines of communication open, offensive coordinator Ron Turner chats up quarterback Rex Grossman at practice.
JIM PRISCHING

# RON TURNER
## OFFENSIVE COORDINATOR:
## the low-key director

Lovie Smith likes to describe the Bears' approach to offense this way: "We get off the bus running."

Indeed, the Bears have been synonymous with a strong running game since the leather-helmeted days of Bronko Nagurski and Red Grange.

But this season they have opted to take an occasional break from smash-mouth and throw the ball around a little, for fun as well as profit.

Under Ron Turner, in the second year of his second tour as offensive coordinator, the Bears have blended Thomas Jones' darting runs with Rex Grossman's pinpoint passing into an attack that's as versatile as it is productive, as balanced as any in football.

"Ron has put us in a system that he really believes in, so we're going to believe in it," veteran center Olin Kreutz says.

Turner grew up in Martinez, Calif., and got his start in coaching at the University of the Pacific in Stockton, so it's no surprise that he's a disciple of the pass-happy West Coast offense. But he believes in adapting his scheme to the talents of his players

rather than trying to force things, which was one of unpopular predecessor Terry Shea's flaws.

"His motto is 'Let the players make plays,' and that's all he tries to do," says Kurt Kittner, quarterback for the Illinois team Turner coached to a Big Ten championship and a Sugar Bowl berth in 2001.

Turner has, in essence, reinvented the tight end position for the Bears, turning Desmond Clark into a productive receiver in a spread-the-wealth scheme that often has seven or eight players catching passes. No one has benefited more from Turner's approach than Grossman, the fourth-year quarterback who seems headed for a Pro Bowl, finally blessed with good health and a system he believes in.

"Coach Turner and I are on the same page," Grossman says. "He does a great job calling plays according to how the flow of the game is going. He's going to make the appropriate call at any given time. We go into each game with a balanced attack." His players take it from there.

—*Dan McGrath*

# 8

# REX GROSSMAN

## QUARTERBACK: the emerging standout

In his fourth season, Rex Grossman finally got to play four games. In every previous year, he was limited by injuries, first a finger, then a knee, then an ankle. He had never started more than three games in a season, so it wasn't until midway through his fourth year that he had started the equivalent of one full 16-game season.

The results were spectacular and predictable, a string of impressive outings interrupted by befuddling lapses. On balance, Grossman left little doubt that his potential, if not always his performance, was worth the patience of general manager Jerry Angelo and coach Lovie Smith.

The Bears had not seen such hope for the future of the quarterback position since Jim McMahon arrived in 1982. Like Grossman, McMahon battled injury problems, but he also guided the 1985 Super Bowl team.

In a lackluster exhibition season, Grossman heard boos amid calls for new backup Brian Griese, who put up better passing numbers. But Smith and offensive coordinator Ron Turner never wavered in their belief that Grossman was their man, and Grossman never wavered in his confidence.

"My major goal is to win the Super Bowl," Grossman says. "And the only way a player can say 'I told you so' is to win it."

Through the disappointment of the injuries and the disapproval of skeptics, Grossman maintained poise and class, displaying maturity and perspective necessary to long-term success at his position. He never failed to give credit to teammates and coaches when things went right and made no excuses when they didn't.

Grossman admits he is "living a dream" by quarterbacking an NFL team. Having grown up in Bloomington, Ind., before starting for three years at Florida, his Midwest roots appear to make him the ideal fit for the Bears.

— *Don Pierson*

Whether on the field or charging out of the locker room, Rex Grossman is assuming a position of leadership. HEATHER STONE

# CONVERSATION
## with Rex Grossman

The 6-foot-1-inch, 217-pounder played at Florida, where he was the Heisman Trophy runner-up and Associated Press National Player of the Year in 2001.

**Favorite college team growing up:** "Indiana. I went to about every single basketball and football game growing up."

**Favorite football player growing up:** "Jim Harbaugh and Brett Favre. Those guys I looked up to and really liked watching."

**What's on the iPod when you work out?** "It's a pretty eclectic mix, from house music to rap to Bob Marley to Dave Matthews Band, anything that I'm in the mood for at that given time."

**Toughest loss you've ever had as a player:** "Had a few tough losses. In college we lost to Tennessee with an opportunity to go to the national championship game. And then to lose last year in the playoffs was a bad feeling as well. The opportunity we had was right there, if we were to win that game, then go on to the NFC championship game with an opportunity to go to the Super Bowl, that's the ultimate."

**Toughest rivalry you've been a part of:** "Florida-Florida State. I'd love to say the Packers, but we've done pretty well against the Packers, so …"

**Word is your folks have never missed one of your games. That true?** "That's still true. … They'd fly down [to Florida] every Friday night and come see the game, no matter if it was in Starkville, Miss., on the road in the SEC or whatever. I've had great family support throughout my whole football career."

**Rex Grossman has sometimes battled inconsistency but has shown a strong arm in the 2006 season.** HEATHER STONE

# 87

# MUHSIN MUHAMMAD

## WIDE RECEIVER: the steady veteran

MOOOOOOSE!

The endearing chant from Bears fans reverberates throughout Soldier Field every time veteran wide receiver Muhsin Muhammad catches a pass. And that means there have been a lot of hoarse fans the last couple of seasons.

Muhammad began his NFL career when Carolina made him its second-round selection, 43rd overall, out of Michigan State in 1996. With Carolina, Muhammad established himself as a big-time receiver in 2000 by topping the NFC and tying for the NFL lead in receptions with a career-high and franchise-record 102 for 1,183 yards and six touchdowns. He went on to become Carolina's all-time receptions leader.

The Bears acquired the two-time Pro Bowl selection on Feb. 27, 2005, and signed him to a six-year contract.

An all-state linebacker and running back at Waverly High School in Lansing, Mich., Muhammad earned three letters in football, two in basketball and two in track before heading off to Michigan State, where he became a receiver.

Rex Grossman used Muhammad as his favorite target in 2005 before the young Bears quarterback got hurt. In 2006, Grossman has a relative embarrassment of riches when it comes to receivers to distribute the ball.

"It's fun in a regular set to have Desmond Clark, Bernard Berrian and Moose," Grossman says. "Those guys are playing really, really well."

Muhammad not only plays a pretty good game, he talks one as well. The Chicago/Midwest Emmy nominations came out last fall, and Muhammad was nominated for his work on the "Hangin' with the Moose" segment that appeared on Comcast SportsNet's "SportsNite" during the 2005 season.

In 2006, Muhammad once again is seen on Comcast on his own show, "Countdown to Kickoff with Muhsin Muhammad."

His first name is Arabic for "charitable" or "one who does good deeds." He and wife Christa have three daughters—Jordan Taylor, Chase Soen and Kennedy Rain—and one son, Muhsin III.

— *Fred Mitchell*

# 88

# DESMOND CLARK
## TIGHT END: the versatile contributor

The Bears like their tight ends to do lots of different things: run pass routes, block for running backs, help protect their quarterback.

For this kind of multitasking, they found the right man in Desmond Clark.

The 6-foot-3-inch, 249-pound Clark signed as a free agent in 2003. He starred in high school in Lakeland, Fla., playing quarterback and free safety and serving as the holder for former Bears kicker Paul Edinger. He also started three seasons as a guard on the basketball team and played baseball as a senior.

At Wake Forest, Clark was a starting wide receiver. So naturally he became a tight end in the NFL, selected by Denver in the sixth round of the 1999 draft after finishing his college career as the all-time leading receiver in the Atlantic Coast Conference.

But his move to tight end in the pro game has made use of his multiple talents, and in the West Coast offense that the Bears and Broncos run, he has become a weapon.

For Clark, the Bears' offense is proving a perfect fit.

"In this offense, I don't think it's just going to be one impact player," Clark says. "Last year it was just the running back or whatever. We know [Muhsin Muhammad] is going to be an impact player, but the ball is going to be spread around.

"We feel like now everybody is going to play a decent role in the offense—the fullback catching the ball, more than one back running the ball. That's a harder offense to guard against when you've got more than one guy featured. If it's one guy, they can double-team that guy, and then the offense strains to make a play."

— *John Mullin*

# 20
# THOMAS JONES
## RUNNING BACK: the tireless worker

Determined and relentless.

Both words accurately describe the life and football career of Bears running back Thomas Jones.

Since joining the team as a free agent in 2004, Jones has been the central figure in the Bears' offense, rushing for a career-high 1,335 yards in 2005 and playing so well overall that top draft pick Cedric Benson hasn't been seeing the field regularly.

Jones joined Hall of Famer Walter Payton as the only Bears running backs to gain at least 1,300 yards in a season.

Jones' work ethic is the stuff of legend in the Bears' locker room, and his citizenship makes him a role model for younger teammates. In a gesture of appreciation to the University of Virginia, alma mater of Jones and three of his six siblings, he established the Thomas Quinn Jones Scholarship this year at the school in Charlottesville.

"It makes me feel good that I'm going to help someone else have the opportunity to go there," Jones says. "I'm never going to forget where I came from because that's my roots, what made me what I am. I will always show my appreciation."

Two of Jones' sisters, Knetris and Knetta, also attended Virginia. Two other sisters, Gwen and Beatrice, attended Tennessee.

A fifth Jones child, younger brother Julius, was a football standout at Notre Dame and now starts for the Cowboys.

Jones grew up in Big Stone Gap, Va., where his parents worked in the coal mines to provide for their seven children. Betty Jones was a supervisor on the night shift.

"Our sons were able to use their athletic talents to gain scholarships," Betty Jones says. "But football lasts only a few years, and education lasts forever."

All seven Jones kids embraced their parents' values.

"My mom and dad ... emphasized getting A's and B's in school," Jones says. "We wanted to make sure we had something to fall back on in case football didn't work out.

"My parents did a really good job keeping all seven of us focused."

— *Fred Mitchell*

Thomas Jones attempts to hurdle Eric Green in the first quarter of a game that left the Cardinals stunned. JOHN SMIERCIAK

Thomas Jones bulls his way for some of the 111 yards he gained in the victory over San Francisco.
CHARLES CHERNEY

# CONVERSATION
## with Thomas Jones

The 5-foot-10-inch, 215-pound running back was drafted seventh overall by Arizona in 2000 out of Virginia, where he got his psychology degree in 1999 and spent his senior year taking graduate school classes.

**Favorite pro team growing up:** "Bears."

**Favorite college team growing up:** "Tennessee."

**Favorite non-football sport to play:** "Basketball."

**Favorite player growing up:** "Walter Payton."

**What's on the iPod when you work out?** "Cam'ron, Jay Z, G-Unit."

**Toughest one-on-one matchup you've ever faced:** "Junior Seau."

**Favorite game you've ever played in:** "When I had 462 yards in a high school game junior year."

**Toughest loss you've ever had as a player:** "UVa.-Georgia Tech, up 38-17 after three quarters, lost 41-38."

**Favorite team right now not named Bears:** "I don't watch other sports."

**Best advice you ever received:** "Hard work pays off."

**TV show you can't miss:** "The Cosby Show in syndication."

**Favorite movie:** "Sling Blade."

# 80
# BERNARD BERRIAN
## WIDE RECEIVER: the deep threat

Exceptional speed is one of the intangibles that cannot be taught to a receiver. Other key qualities, such as good hands and efficient route running, can be refined with hard work.

Bernard Berrian has been putting all those ingredients together as he gains experience in the NFL.

Hampered by injuries his first couple of years in the league, Berrian was determined to contribute significantly in 2006. His ability to stretch the field as a deep threat for quarterback Rex Grossman allows the tight ends and running backs to become more involved in the pass offense across the middle of the field and in the flat.

The Bears' third-round selection and 78th overall out of Fresno State in the 2004 draft, the 6-foot-1-inch, 185-pound Berrian also has seen time returning kickoffs and punts.

As a receiver, Berrian figures to become better with advice from veterans such as teammate Muhsin Muhammad.

"You can learn a lot from Moose—how to practice, how to study film, how to run routes and how to stay patient," Berrian said. "I don't know if he wants to be looked at as a role model. But he's definitely a guy you can look to for direction."

While defenders might concentrate on more established Bears receivers such as Muhammad, Berrian has been doing his best to make big plays.

"A lot of people go unheard of, and then everyone says, 'Wow, he's a really good player.' Sometimes it's just about getting those opportunities," Berrian said.

"I'm pretty sure opponents know about me, but you still have to worry about Moose on the other side. You still have to worry about the running game, and with Rex throwing the ball, he's liable to throw it anytime. You can't focus on one particular guy."

Berrian certainly received his share of attention at Fresno State, where he was a three-year starter. He wound up his career as the school record-holder in several receiving categories. He finished with 199 receptions for 2,849 yards and 25 touchdowns.

—*Fred Mitchell*

# 63
# ROBERTO GARZA
## GUARD: the bulldozing blocker

For a guy with no anterior cruciate ligament in his right knee, guard Roberto Garza sure found firm footing in a hurry in Chicago. In just Garza's first full season as a Bears starter, team leader Olin Kreutz already considers him good enough to join him in Hawaii at the end of the season.

"He's playing at an All-Pro level," says Kreutz, who has played in five Pro Bowls.

Garza earned the starting right guard job near the end of last season when Terrence Metcalf got hurt. He never gave it back, excelling at run-blocking and communicating well enough with his fellow linemen to keep the blitzers and grass stains off quarterback Rex Grossman.

The Bears recognized the progress Garza showed by locking him up last January with a six-year contract extension.

"These guys play at such a high level that you just have to make sure you're not the weak link," Garza says of playing on a veteran offensive line. "That's a lot of pressure for me. I feel it."

He handles it with an engaging personality that makes him approachable in the locker room and popular in the community. Few Bears stay more active volunteering their time on days off than Garza, whose presence opens a door to a Hispanic audience that isn't traditionally accessible to the NFL. He is one of 19 Hispanic players in the league and appears regularly on Spanish-language TV and radio shows in Chicago, where he converses easily with the hosts.

Not bad for a kid from a small, largely Hispanic town in Texas called Rio Hondo, with less than 2,000 residents. Every Dec. 2 back in his hometown, "Roberto Garza Day" is celebrated.

That gives the locals an opportunity to express their pride in a player who came to the Bears via free agency. General manager Jerry Angelo signed Garza in March 2005 after the Texas A&M-Kingsville product spent his first four seasons in the league as a part-time starter for Atlanta.

Even with six seasons' experience, he is the youngest member of a veteran offensive line many take for granted. He doesn't.

"I'm trying to pick up stuff all the time from these guys, and I do every week," Garza says. "It's such a pleasure."

— *David Haugh*

# 57
# OLIN KREUTZ
## CENTER: the trusted general

Olin Kreutz might just be one of the most self-deprecating players in the NFL. And for a five-time Pro Bowler, this can't be easy.

Calling himself "junk" and playing down his leadership role on the Bears, the veteran center would seemingly much rather skulk around the locker room with a mischievous glint in his eye than talk about himself.

But backup quarterback Kyle Orton puts Kreutz's enormous influence in its proper perspective when he says, "In this locker room, if you have the approval of Olin, everybody will take you in."

More than even cold, hard cash, Kreutz is generally credited with the Bears attracting top-line free-agent linemen such as Ruben Brown and John Tait. And if football can be likened to the proverbial foxhole, most Bears are glad they're in one with Kreutz.

"He has their backs," Bears offensive line coach Harry Hiestand says. "It's never about him. He'll fool around and raise a little hell and deflect some of the other things. But day in and day out, he's the guy getting the job done, he's the guy in charge, he's the guy who keeps everyone focused on what direction we're going."

Former Bears offensive lineman Chris Villarrial, who left in 2003 and is now with the Buffalo Bills, said he still misses Kreutz.

"Every single day, trust me," he says. "He came out every day in practice and played like it was a game. Some guys would be like, `Here we go again,' but not Olin."

Now in his ninth NFL season, that direction is decidedly upward for Kreutz after enduring six losing seasons in his first seven years. A third-round draft pick who came out after his junior season at Washington, the 6-foot-2-inch, 292-pound Kreutz recently signed a three-year contract extension for close to $17.5 million that he said would ensure he will retire as a Bear.

"Honestly, I never expected it to be this good," he said after the 11-5 campaign in 2005. "I enjoy every minute of being here. I've enjoyed my career, and as long as it lasts, I'll always enjoy it."

— *Melissa Isaacson*

Right down the line: Fred Miller (left), Roberto Garza, Olin Kreutz, Ruben Brown and John Tait rest in the 49ers game. CHARLES CHERNEY

SCOTT STRAZZANTE

# CONVERSATION
## with Olin Kreutz

A teammate once called Kreutz "the perfect rookie." Why? "I didn't talk at all. I don't believe rookies should talk. I think you have to earn your respect, and that's what I tried to do.

**On being from Hawaii and living there in the off-season:** "When you're from Hawaii, it's hard to live anywhere else. But this is my job, and they pay me a lot of |money to stay in Chicago."

**On marriage to wife Wendi:** "It's great. It's everything I expected it to be and more. It's been fun."

**On his three children:** "I hope they don't give me as much trouble as I gave my parents."

**On his family:** "My mom and my whole family will always be a big influence in my life. My family is very down to earth."

**On his mentors:** "Big Cat [Williams] and Chris Villarrial weren't two of my mentors, they were my mentors. They taught me how to be professional."

**On playing the game:** "I care about the team. I care about how I do my job. I care about doing things the right way."

# 32
# CEDRIC BENSON
## RUNNING BACK: the determined backup

That his potential as an NFL running back is still the most impressive thing about the Bears' Cedric Benson is not necessarily a negative.

But Benson would surely say it is. And that says plenty about the second-year player.

Still crying out for playing time after shedding real tears on draft day in 2005 upon being selected by the Bears with the fourth pick, Benson is hoping his best days are still ahead of him.

If so, they will be some good times indeed.

The sixth-leading rusher in NCAA Division I-A history, Benson simply did not know of any life except that of a starter be-fore signing with the Bears. One of three players in NCAA history to rush for 5,000 yards and score 400 points in a career, he started in each of his four seasons at Texas after a high school career in which he was a three-time state offensive player of the year and led his team to three consecutive state titles.

But a contract standoff caused him to miss his first NFL training camp, a mid-season knee injury in his first pro start sidelined him for six games ... and Benson has been playing catch-up ever since.

Now, after a shoulder injury in training camp 2006 once again helped derail his as-pirations of starting, Benson must be con-tent to find his niche behind Thomas Jones.

But that doesn't mean a player can't dream.

"I often daydream about having a good game, having a big game, getting 100 yards or just getting in the groove," Benson says. "But I don't dwell on it."

Even so, the reality is that Benson is not nearly as busy as he would like to be. Head-ing into the second half of this season, the last time he had carried the ball 20 times or more was for Texas in the 2005 Rose Bowl. And he hadn't gained 100 yards in a game since Nov. 26, 2004, when he rushed for 165 yards against Texas A&M.

"My expectations of me are very high," Benson once said. "Every challenge that football poses can only make me better."

— *Melissa Isaacson*

As Brendon Ayanbadejo (94) puts the final block on Arizona's Marcel Shipp, Devin Hester scampers in to score. JIM PRISCHING

# SPECIAL TEAMS

# 9

# ROBBIE GOULD
## KICKER: the unexpected blessing

Robbie Gould was a little low. He was working in a friend's construction business. He'd had a shot with the New England Patriots, but they cut him. He tried the Baltimore Ravens next, but they waived him. Pro football had booted him out.

The Bears also were down. They had lost 20-10 to a weak Cleveland Browns team on Oct. 9, 2005, sliding to 1-3 on the year. Worse yet, kicker Doug Brien had hurt his back during practice and missed the game.

Brien had been a bust. He was 1-for-4 on field goals. Having parted with Paul Edinger, who signed with Minnesota the previous summer, the Bears were in a bind. They invited five kickers to an emergency tryout, one being a 22-year-old Robbie Gould.

"His leg was very strong," coach Lovie Smith says. "I saw that right away."

So the Bears gave the kid from Penn State a shot. They promptly won eight straight games.

Fans knew very little about him. For a while they didn't even know his name was pronounced "Gold." But they became acquainted as Gould made 21 of 27 field goals and led the playoff-bound Bears in scoring.

Gould wasn't overly familiar with Chicago either.

"Except for the wind," he says. "I'd kicked in the Midwest most of my life, but with Chicago you always hear the 'windy' thing."

He was introduced to the wind against the 49ers, when a gust blew a 37-yard attempt like a hot-dog wrapper. It made TV blooper reels from coast to coast.

But this season, Gould has taken the Windy City by storm. He has been money and was voted the NFC's special-teams player of the month for October. After going 2-for-2 against Miami in the Bears' eighth game, Gould had tied Kevin Butler's franchise record of 24 consecutive made field goals dating to last season.

"I don't know where we'd be without him," defensive end Alex Brown says. "Our getting Robbie Gould to kick for us was a total blessing."

And the construction business' loss.

— *Mike Downey*

# 23
# DEVIN HESTER
## SPECIAL-TEAMER: the explosiver returner

Every time Devin Hester heads upfield on a punt return, Bears offensive coaches find themselves shaking their heads and pondering the possibilities.

Hester considers himself a defensive back, in the mold of Deion Sanders, who was his boyhood idol growing up in South Florida. But the rookie from the University of Miami is such an electrifying weapon as a punt returner that the Bears' offensive staff can't help dreaming of what might happen were he to get his hands on the ball more than four or five times a game.

"In two or three years, I could see myself being a receiver, sure," Hester says.

Sanders, after all, spent some time on the offensive side of the ball and also re-turned punts during a Hall of Fame-caliber career. For now, bringing back punts is Hester's primary responsibility. And no one in the NFL has done it better than the 24-year-old second-round pick, who has Gale Sayers-like moves to match his breakaway speed.

At Miami, Hester was known as "Anytime," a salute to his big-play ability to score from anywhere on the field. And he didn't waste any time making an impact for the Bears, bringing a punt back 84 yards for a touchdown in their season-opening 26-0 win over the Green Bay Packers. Hester was the first Bears rookie to score on a punt return in his NFL debut since 1956.

Against Arizona he made a play that's likely to lead the team's 2006 highlight film: an 83-yard return for the go-ahead touchdown as the Bears miraculously erased a 21-point third-quarter deficit and won 24-23.

You'd think teams would get the message and start kicking away from him … but no. He set up a touchdown with a 42-yard return against San Francisco in the Bears' 41-10 laugher.

"I would say returning punts is 20 percent coaching and and 80 percent natural instinct," Hester says. "You can't put just anybody out there. You feel when somebody is up on you, so you don't have to look. It's just something God blesses you with—and I have it."

— *Dan McGrath*

IN THE EARLY 1980s, as the Bears were assembling their eventual Super Bowl championship team, I started to take an interest in photography.

As the youngest member of a sports-crazed family, I often would borrow my dad's camera and wander Soldier Field photographing the faces and places that made the old stadium by the lake unique.

Over the past two decades as I have made a career in the newspaper world, my vantage point has migrated from the 35th row to the 35-yard line.

The downside of that migration has been my increased focus on the action on the field. The tackles and touchdowns have won out over the cheers and beers.

With this photo essay, I once again turn my back on the game to capture the rich and vibrant scene that defines game day at Soldier Field.

# AT SOLDIER FIELD
Photo essay by SCOTT STRAZZANTE

*By* DAVID HAUGH

# WHAT THE BEARS MEAN TO CHICAGO

N A SINGLE WEEK in October, Tickets321 in Chicago sold more than 100 Super Bowl tickets to Bears fans willing to risk enough money for a mortgage payment in the belief their team will be playing Feb. 4 in Miami. The money-is-no-object Bears frenzy makes perfect sense to many who understand the viselike grip the team has on Chicago's heart.

Articulating the allegiance to the Bears can be as tricky as explaining one's devotion to his religion or spouse, even for longtime Chicagoans who understand the city like a dear friend.

"Maybe it's something in the water or the air, but win or lose, the Bears are suffused intrinsically into everything we think, feel and sense about Chicago," said Don Rose, a longtime political consultant dating to Mayor Richard J. Daley. "They make us feel good about ourselves. They are always the Bears, and this is always Chicago. The Bears are us."

Gov. Rod Blagojevich believes the Bears have made themselves so popular since their inception in 1921 because of a style that has stayed consistent and given working Chicagoans an example to follow.

"Chicago has a spirit of hard work, determination and a no-nonsense attitude, and ... the Bears play hard and they work as a team," Blagojevich said. "A lot of fans feel this team could be as great as the 1985 Bears or any of the great teams of the Monsters of the Midway era."

Mike Ditka coached the only Bears Super Bowl winner, and he achieved local immortality. He understands the football fervor he helped create.

"This is the greatest sports town in the world, [but] I always thought this was a North Side town with the Bears and Cubs, and it probably still is," Ditka said. "But the Sox brought a lot of joy. The Bulls brought a lot of joy. In the past years—way back—the Blackhawks brought a lot of joy. We need a winner again, especially in football."

George Halas would be proud but maybe

not surprised, according to Jeff Davis, the author of "Papa Bear." Davis traced the Bears hysteria so obvious today back to Halas.

"It still is the spirit of Halas carrying on nearly a quarter-century after his death [in 1983]," Davis said. "He coached them to more wins than any other team and made [the NFL], through his wit and guile, the richest and most powerful sports organization on earth. It's no coincidence that Chicago responded to this native son and his Bears."

People conditioned to classifying the Bears as playing in a "Black and Blue" division or embodying a smash-mouth persona don't care if the method of winning includes a touch passer and speed rushers. As long as the new Bears win, they conjure up old images.

"Carl Sandburg famously described Chicago as the City of Big Shoulders, and the Chicago Bears personify this spirit, a blue-collar team for a blue-collar town because they are hard workers, hard hitters and diverse," said Newton Minow, a powerful Chicago lawyer still well-known for calling TV a "vast wasteland" in 1961 as chairman of the Federal Communications Commission. "Players like [Sid] Luckman, [Dick] Butkus, [Mike] Singletary, [Walter] Payton and [Gale] Sayers, and more recently [Brian] Urlacher, represent what Chicago is all about. And that's why we love them."

Sayers credits the Bears' trademark tough defenses with creating a lunch-pail identity embraced in a city that likes to consider itself rugged.

"The Bears always have been known for their defense, and people seem to identify with that," Sayers said. "There are White Sox fans and Cubs fans, but this is a Bears town."

The man who runs that town likened the appeal and success of the Bears to good government. Mayor Richard M. Daley, a Bears fan who was instrumental in helping the team obtain financing to renovate Soldier Field, sounded almost envious describing the way Lovie Smith has coaxed his players on both sides of the ball into working together toward a common cause.

"They are playing as a team, and that's what you have to do with the City Council," Daley said. "There will be differences every day with aldermen, but if you don't play as a team and get some things done, then everyone screams and yells and nothing gets done. You have to really work as a team."

MY ESSAY AIMS to have a vintage feel, even though I photographed in the here and now. I tried to capture the shiny aerodynamic sweep of Soldier Field, the lighter, faster team of the future that still retains the gritty hard-nosed tradition of generations of Chicago football. I wanted images that convey a sense of history standing still, with the smell of brats grilling, your shoes sticky with spilled beer and the feel of the wind blowing off the lake on a Sunday afternoon.

# ON THE SIDELINES
## Photo essay by E. JASON WAMBSGANS

# THE 2006 CHICAGO BEARS ROSTER

| | PLAYER | POSITION | COLLEGE | HEIGHT | WEIGHT | YEARS IN NFL | AGE |
|---|---|---|---|---|---|---|---|
| 97 | Anderson, Mark | Defensive end | Alabama | 6-4 | 255 | ROOKIE | 23 |
| 94 | Ayanbadejo, Brendon | Linebacker | UCLA | 6-1 | 228 | 4 | 30 |
| 32 | Benson, Cedric | Running back | Texas | 5-11 | 220 | 2 | 23 |
| 80 | Berrian, Bernard | Wide receiver | Fresno State | 6-1 | 185 | 3 | 25 |
| 70 | Boone, Alfonso | Defensive tackle | Mt. San Antonio JC | 6-4 | 318 | 6 | 30 |
| 16 | Bradley, Mark | Wide receiver | Oklahoma | 6-2 | 198 | 2 | 24 |
| 55 | Briggs, Lance | Linebacker | Arizona | 6-1 | 240 | 4 | 25 |
| 96 | Brown, Alex | Defensive end | Florida | 6-3 | 260 | 5 | 27 |
| 30 | Brown, Mike | Strong safety | Nebraska | 5-10 | 207 | 7 | 28 |
| 74 | Brown, Ruben | Guard | Pittsburgh | 6-3 | 300 | 12 | 34 |
| 72 | Bryan, Copeland | Defensive end | Arizona | 6-3 | 253 | ROOKIE | 23 |
| 88 | Clark, Desmond | Tight end | Wake Forest | 6-3 | 249 | 8 | 29 |
| 17 | Currie, Airese | Wide receiver | Clemson | 5-11 | 185 | 1 | 23 |
| 81 | Davis, Rashied | Wide receiver | San Jose State | 5-9 | 183 | 2 | 27 |
| 98 | Dvoracek, Dusty | Defensive tackle | Oklahoma | 6-3 | 305 | ROOKIE | 23 |
| 22 | Everett, Tyler | Strong safety | Ohio State | 5-11 | 202 | ROOKIE | 23 |
| 12 | Gage, Justin | Wide receiver | Missouri | 6-4 | 212 | 4 | 25 |
| 90 | Garay, Antonio | Defensive tackle | Boston College | 6-4 | 303 | 2 | 26 |
| 63 | Garza, Roberto | Guard | Texas A&M-Kingsville | 6-2 | 305 | 6 | 27 |
| 85 | Gilmore, John | Tight end | Penn State | 6-5 | 257 | 5 | 27 |
| 9 | Gould, Robbie | Kicker | Penn State | 6-0 | 183 | 2 | 24 |
| 14 | Griese, Brian | Quarterback | Michigan | 6-3 | 214 | 9 | 31 |
| 8 | Grossman, Rex | Quarterback | Florida | 6-1 | 217 | 4 | 26 |
| 46 | Harris, Chris | Free safety | Louisiana-Monroe | 6-0 | 205 | 2 | 24 |
| 91 | Harris, Tommie | Defensive tackle | Oklahoma | 6-3 | 295 | 3 | 23 |
| 83 | Hass, Mike | Wide receiver | Oregon State | 6-1 | 209 | ROOKIE | 23 |
| 23 | Hester, Devin | Cornerback | Miami | 5-11 | 186 | ROOKIE | 24 |
| 92 | Hillenmeyer, Hunter | Linebacker | Vanderbilt | 6-4 | 238 | 4 | 26 |
| 71 | Idonije, Israel | Defensive tackle | Manitoba | 6-6 | 270 | 3 | 25 |
| 53 | Joe, Leon | Linebacker | Maryland | 6-1 | 230 | 3 | 25 |
| 47 | Johnson, Bryan | Fullback | Boise State | 6-1 | 244 | 6 | 28 |
| 99 | Johnson, Tank | Defensive tackle | Washington | 6-3 | 300 | 3 | 24 |
| 35 | Johnson, Todd | Strong safety | Florida | 6-1 | 200 | 3 | 27 |
| 20 | Jones, Thomas | Running back | Virginia | 5-10 | 215 | 7 | 28 |
| 89 | Joppru, Bennie | Tight end | Michigan | 6-4 | 242 | 4 | 26 |
| 57 | Kreutz, Olin | Center | Washington | 6-2 | 292 | 9 | 29 |
| 75 | LeVoir, Mark | Tackle | Notre Dame | 6-7 | 310 | ROOKIE | 24 |
| 65 | Mannelly, Patrick | Long snapper | Duke | 6-5 | 265 | 9 | 31 |
| 38 | Manning, Danieal | Free safety | Abilene Christian | 5-11 | 196 | ROOKIE | 24 |

| PLAYER | | POSITION | COLLEGE | HEIGHT | WEIGHT | YEARS IN NFL | AGE |
|---|---|---|---|---|---|---|---|
| 24 | Manning Jr., Ricky | Cornerback | UCLA | 5-9 | 188 | 4 | 25 |
| 4 | Maynard, Brad | Punter | Ball State | 6-1 | 186 | 10 | 32 |
| 58 | McClover, Darrell | Linebacker | Miami | 6-2 | 226 | 3 | 25 |
| 36 | McGowan, Brandon | Strong safety | Maine | 5-11 | 205 | 2 | 23 |
| 37 | McKie, Jason | Fullback | Temple | 5-11 | 243 | 5 | 26 |
| 60 | Metcalf, Terrence | Guard | Mississippi | 6-3 | 318 | 5 | 28 |
| 69 | Miller, Fred | Tackle | Baylor | 6-7 | 314 | 11 | 33 |
| 87 | Muhammad, Muhsin | Wide receiver | Michigan State | 6-2 | 215 | 11 | 33 |
| 68 | Oakley, Anthony | Guard/center | Western Kentucky | 6-4 | 298 | 1 | 25 |
| 93 | Ogunleye, Adewale | Defensive end | Indiana | 6-4 | 260 | 6 | 29 |
| 18 | Orton, Kyle | Quarterback | Purdue | 6-4 | 217 | 2 | 23 |
| 29 | Peterson, Adrian | Running back | Georgia Southern | 5-10 | 210 | 5 | 27 |
| 64 | Reed, Tyler | Guard | Penn State | 6-4 | 307 | ROOKIE | 24 |
| 82 | Reid, Gabe | Tight end | Brigham Young | 6-3 | 252 | 4 | 29 |
| 84 | Rideau, Brandon | Wide receiver | Kansas | 6-3 | 200 | 2 | 24 |
| 48 | Runnels, J.D. | Fullback | Oklahoma | 5-11 | 240 | ROOKIE | 22 |
| 95 | Scott, Ian | Defensive tackle | Florida | 6-3 | 302 | 4 | 25 |
| 78 | St. Clair, John | Tackle | Virginia | 6-5 | 315 | 7 | 29 |
| 76 | Tait, John | Tackle | Brigham Young | 6-6 | 312 | 8 | 31 |
| 33 | Tillman, Charles | Cornerback | Louisiana-Lafayette | 6-1 | 196 | 4 | 25 |
| 54 | Urlacher, Brian | Linebacker | New Mexico | 6-4 | 258 | 7 | 28 |
| 31 | Vasher, Nathan | Cornerback | Texas | 5-10 | 180 | 3 | 24 |
| 21 | Wesley, Dante | Cornerback | Arkansas-Pine Bluff | 6-1 | 210 | 5 | 27 |
| 52 | Williams, Jamar | Linebacker | Arizona State | 6-0 | 234 | ROOKIE | 22 |
| 59 | Wilson, Rod | Linebacker | South Carolina | 6-2 | 230 | 1 | 24 |
| 44 | Worrell, Cameron | Strong safety | Fresno State | 5-11 | 194 | 3 | 26 |

ROSTER INCLUDES PRACTICE SQUAD AND INJURED-RESERVE LIST

## COACHES

**Smith, Lovie**    Head coach

### DEFENSE
**Rivera, Ron**    Defensive coordinator
**Babich, Bob**    Asst. head coach/linebackers
**Johnson, Don**    Defensive line
**Wilks, Steven**    Defensive backs
**Lee, Lloyd**    Defensive assistant
**Byrd, Gill**    Defensive quality control

### OFFENSE
**Turner, Ron**    Offensive coordinator
**Boras, Rob**    Tight ends
**Drake, Darryl**    Wide receivers
**Goodwin, Harold**    Assistant offensive line
**Hiestand, Harry**    Offensive line
**Spencer, Tim**    Running backs
**Wilson, Wade**    Quarterbacks
**Bajakian, Mike**    Offensive quality control

### SPECIAL TEAMS
**Toub, Dave**    Special teams coordinator
**O'Dea, Kevin**    Assistant special teams coach

### STRENGTH AND CONDITIONING
**Jones, Rusty**    Coordinator
**Arthur, Jim**    Assistant

## Chicago Tribune

# BEARS ROAR

**MEET THE MEN WHO PUT THE SWAGGER BACK INTO CHICAGO FOOTBALL**

**PUBLISHER** Scott Smith
**EDITOR** Ann Marie Lipinski
**MANAGING EDITOR, NEWS** George de Lama
**MANAGING EDITOR, FEATURES** James Warren

**SPORTS EDITORS** Dan McGrath, Bill Adee
**PHOTO EDITORS** Torry Bruno,
Todd Panagopoulos, Robin Daughtridge,
Keith Swinden
**WRITERS** David Haugh, John Mullin,
Don Pierson, Melissa Isaacson, Fred Mitchell,
Dan McGrath, Rahula Strohl
**COPY EDITORS** Tom Carkeek, Mike Sansone,
Lee Gordon, Ed Cavanaugh, Bob Fischer,
Mark Shapiro, Mike Pankow, Mike Kellams
**ART DIRECTORS** Chuck Burke, Joan Cairney
**IMAGING** John Andersen, Bill Avorio,
Don Bierman, Christine Bruno, Kathy Celer,
Jennifer Fletcher, Peggy Huber, Beth Kovach,
Hung T. Vu, Min Pak
**PROJECT MANAGERS**
Bill Parker, Susan Zukrow

**Adewale Ogunleye (93) shows that Jon Kitna's jersey is made with stretchable material, sacking the Lions quarterback with help from Brian Urlacher (54) and Alex Brown (96).**
NUCCIO DINUZZO

**JIM PRISCHING**